Big and Dangerous Bulls

Written by
Michèle Dufresne

Here is a bull.
The bull is not small at all.
He is big!
tail
leg

Cows are female and bulls are male.
eye
head
horn
ear
nose
mouth
hoof

What can the bull do?

He can pull a big **cart**.

Pull! Pull! Pull!

The bull is going to roll
in the grass.
He wants to get rid of the
bugs on his back!

You must have a tall wall or **fence** for a bull. Bulls are big and can jump over a small fence or wall.

A sturdy fence keeps the bull safe and stops it from running away. A good fence keeps the bull and people safe!

Can you see the bull?

The **farmer** calls to the bull,

"Come here, bull!"

The bull is in his stall.
Look at the **hay**.
Yum! Yum!
A bull eats hay, grass, and grains like corn and oats. It also needs fresh water every day.

glossary

cart

fence

farmer

hay